Creative PIANO SOLO

JAZZ STANDARDS

Unique, Distinctive Piano Arrangements of 20 Classics

ISBN 978-1-5400-3528-8

Visit Hal Leonard Online at
www.halleonard.com

Contact us:
Hal Leonard
7777 West Bluemound Road
Milwaukee, WI 53213
Email: info@halleonard.com

In Europe, contact:
Hal Leonard Europe Limited
42 Wigmore Street
Marylebone, London, W1U 2RN
Email: info@halleonardeurope.com

In Australia, contact:
Hal Leonard Australia Pty. Ltd.
4 Lentara Court
Cheltenham, Victoria, 3192 Australia
Email: info@halleonard.com.au

ALL THE THINGS YOU ARE

from VERY WARM FOR MAY

Lyrics by OSCAR HAMMERSTEIN II
Music by JEROME KERN

Medium Swing

Bright Swing

BEYOND THE SEA

Lyrics by JACK LAWRENCE
Music by CHARLES TRENET and ALBERT LASRY
Original French Lyric to "La Mer" by CHARLES TRENET

Pedal ad lib.

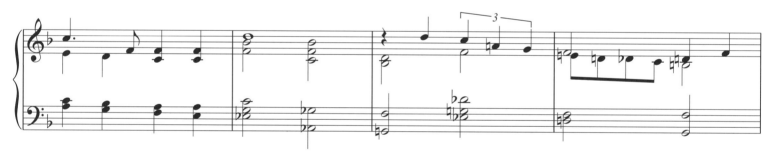

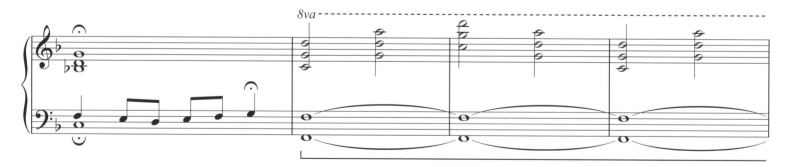

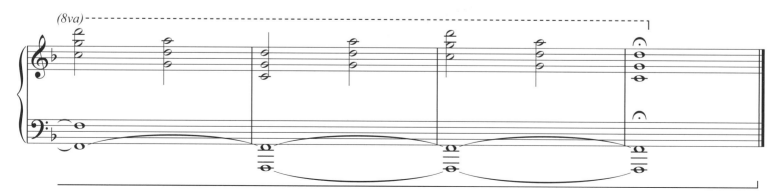

BUT BEAUTIFUL

Words by JOHNNY BURKE
Music by JIMMY VAN HEUSEN

Moderately slow, expressively

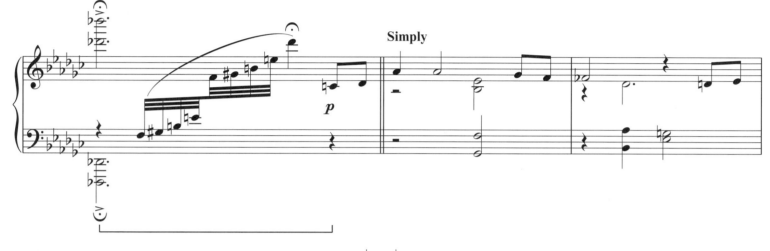

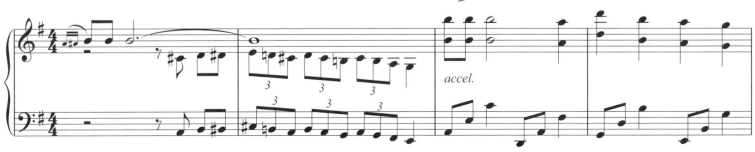

BLUE SKIES

from BETSY

Words and Music by
IRVING BERLIN

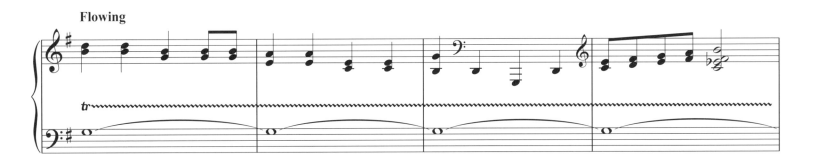

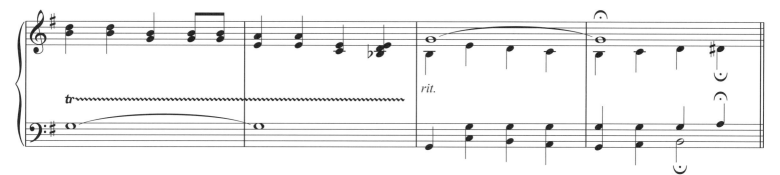

Moderate Swing

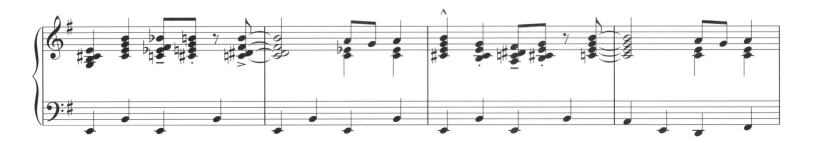

DREAM

Words and Music by
JOHNNY MERCER

Moderate Swing

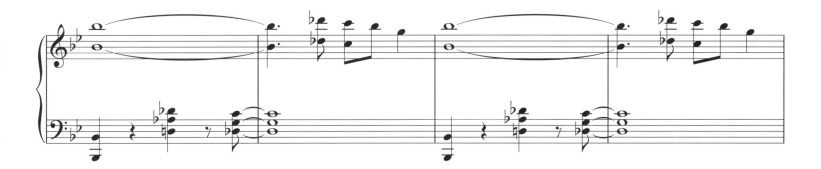

GEORGIA ON MY MIND

Words by STUART GORRELL
Music by HOAGY CARMICHAEL

Straight 8ths   *8va* ⌐⌐   **Fast Bossa**

rit.

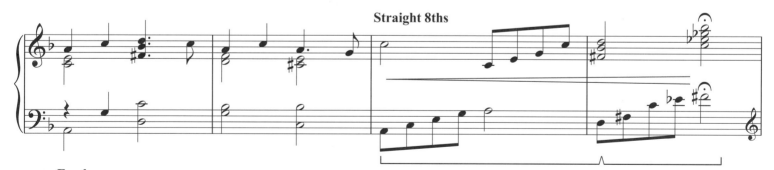

HERE'S THAT RAINY DAY

Words by JOHNNY BURKE
Music by JIMMY VAN HEUSEN

Gentle Bossa Nova

Flowing

THE LADY IS A TRAMP
from BABES IN ARMS

Words by LORENZ HART
Music by RICHARD RODGERS

Moderately fast Swing

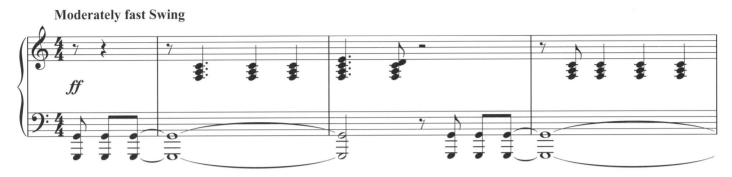

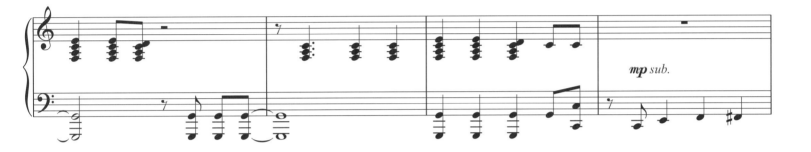

Pedal ad lib.

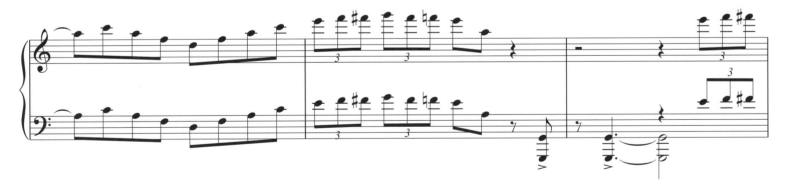

mp   *legato*

Pedal ad lib.

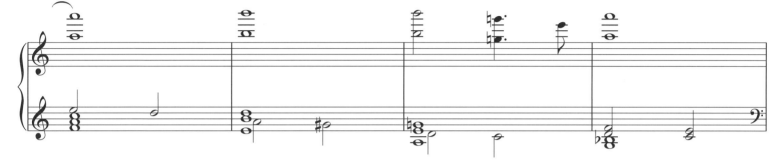

f

Straight 8ths

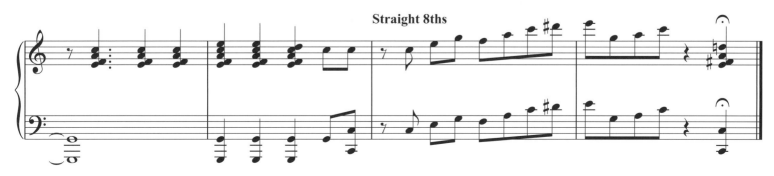

I CONCENTRATE ON YOU
from BROADWAY MELODY OF 1940

Words and Music by
COLE PORTER

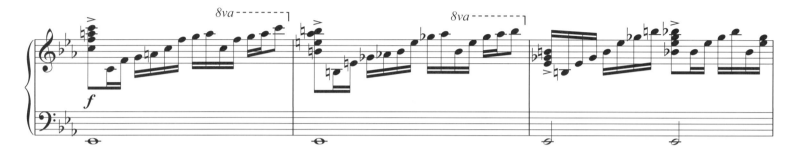

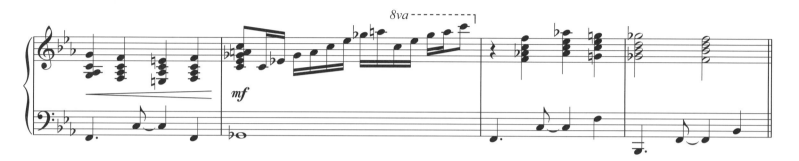

IN THE WEE SMALL HOURS
OF THE MORNING

Words by BOB HILLIARD
Music by DAVID MANN

Moderately bright Swing

Expressively (♫ = ♫)

Swing

D.S. al Coda

CODA

LIKE SOMEONE IN LOVE

Words by JOHNNY BURKE
Music by JIMMY VAN HEUSEN

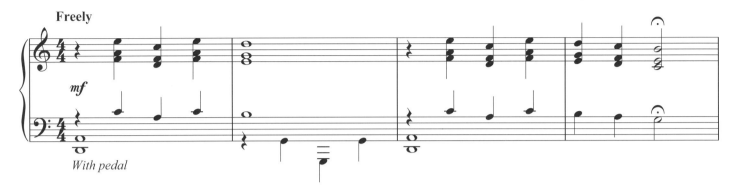

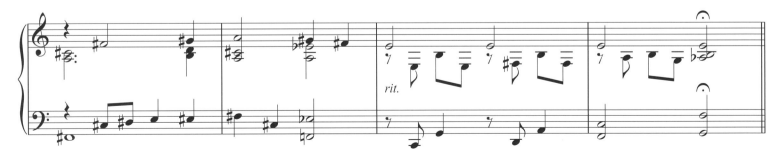

Moderately fast Swing

To Coda ⊕

D.S. al Coda

CODA

Broadly, straight 8ths

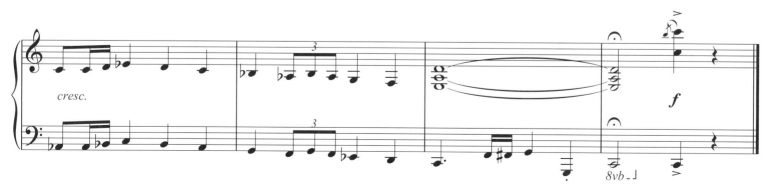

SKYLARK

Words by JOHNNY MERCER
Music by HOAGY CARMICHAEL

Slowly, straight 8ths

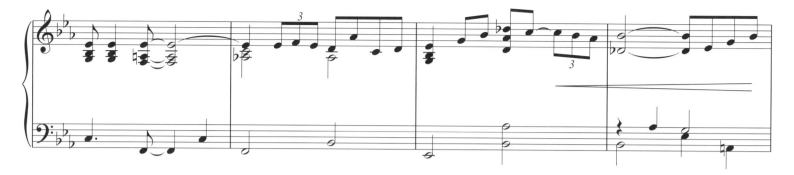

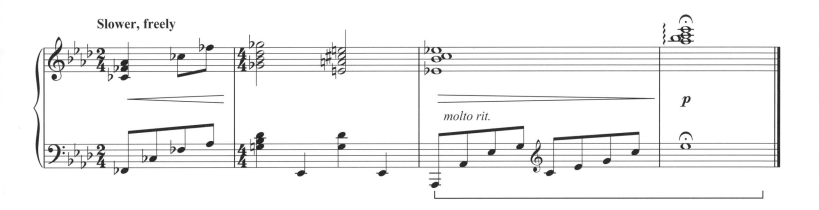

LITTLE GIRL BLUE
from JUMBO

Words by LORENZ HART
Music by RICHARD RODGERS

Slowly, expressively

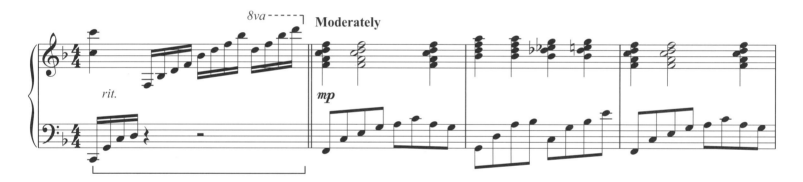

Medium Stride, a little faster

Straight 8ths

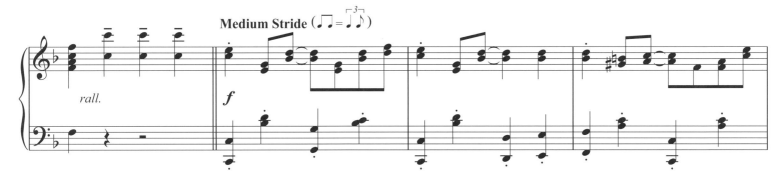

Jazz Waltz

Con moto, straight 8ths

A NIGHTINGALE SANG
IN BERKELEY SQUARE

Lyric by ERIC MASCHWITZ
Music by MANNING SHERWIN

Moderate Jazz Waltz

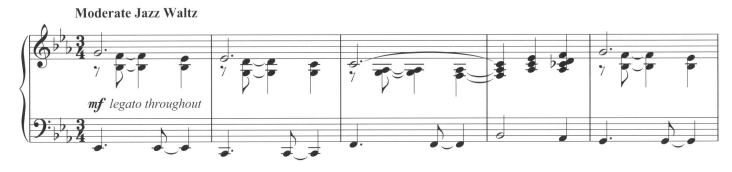

D.S. al Coda

CODA

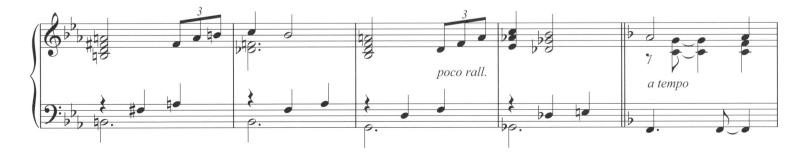

poco rall.

a tempo

dim. poco a poco

pp

8vb

SOMEONE TO WATCH OVER ME

from OH, KAY!

Music and Lyrics by GEORGE GERSHWIN
and IRA GERSHWIN

Medium slow, very expressively

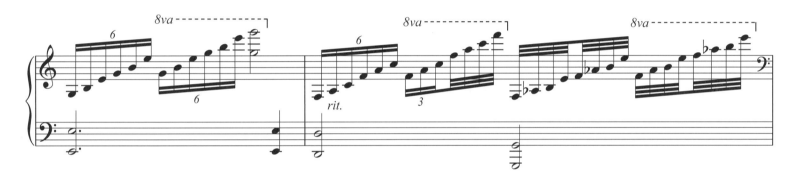

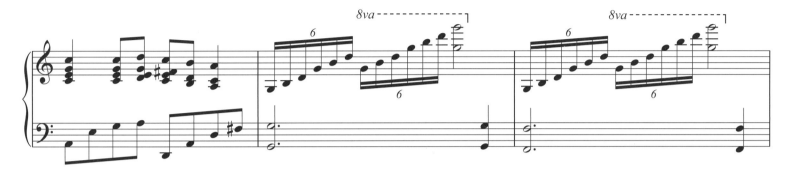

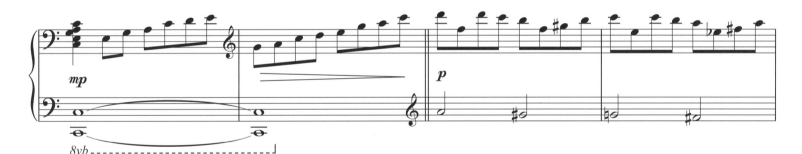

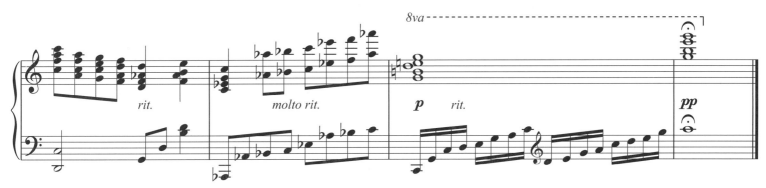

TEACH ME TONIGHT

Words by SAMMY CAHN
Music by GENE DE PAUL

Moderately, evenly

Shuffle 16ths

Straight 16ths

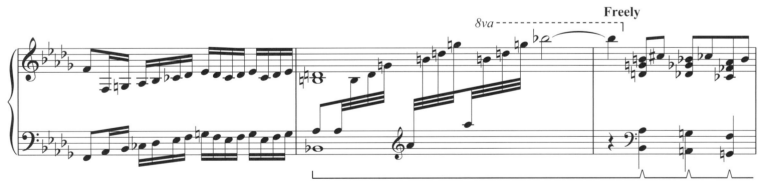

THAT'S ALL

Words and Music by BOB HAYMES
and ALAN E. BRANDT

65

To Coda $\oplus$

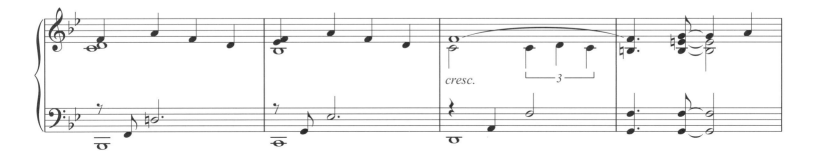

D.S. al Coda

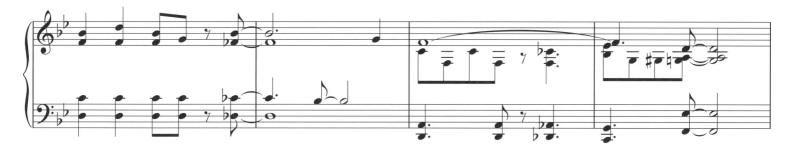

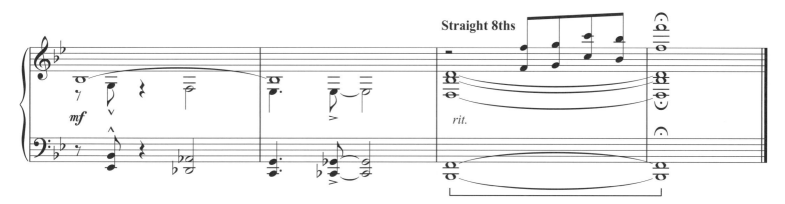

THE VERY THOUGHT OF YOU

Words and Music by
RAY NOBLE

Slowly, expressively

pp

Pedal ad lib. throughout

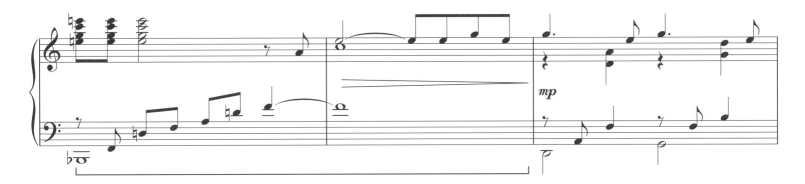

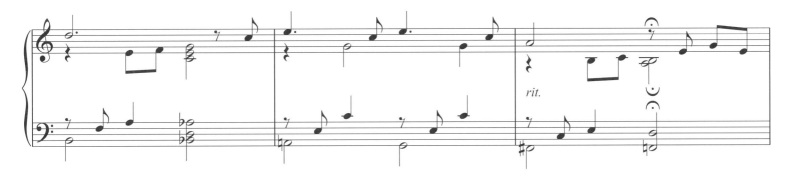

WHAT'LL I DO?
from MUSIC BOX REVUE OF 1924

Words and Music by
IRVING BERLIN

Slowly, freely

With pedal

Moderate Swing Waltz

Slowly, freely (straight 8ths)

With pedal

Moderate Swing Waltz

rit.

Straight 8ths

rit.

YOU ARE TOO BEAUTIFUL
from HALLELUJAH, I'M A BUM

Words by LORENZ HART
Music by RICHARD RODGERS

Soulfully